HERE'S A QUESTION

?

STARTING
THE FAMILY CONVERSATION

ISBN 978-0-9971606-0-4

Here's a Question
www.heresaquestion.org

Special thanks to Kobus Johnsen

TO ADDIE, MILLIE, CHARLIE AND CROSBY

Here's a question…

"What's going on in that mind of yours?"

That is the question my wife and I pondered many times as we talked with our children. I am a dad and, by default, I have no idea how to communicate, but I wanted to know what was in the minds and hearts of my children. What makes them who they are? What passions and desires are waiting to be unlocked inside of them? We have three very different children, all who communicate in different ways. At the dinner table, our first-born girl would prefer to dictate the conversation. Our middle boy doesn't want to speak or share at all. Our third, a boy as well, just wants to be the loudest and get the most laughs. It can feel as though we are spending time together, but not really learning about each other. Faced with a challenge, I thought, "We need a plan to get us all talking and learning more about each other. There is good stuff in those little heads and I want to get it out!" Thus, I started writing questions for us to discuss as a family. Suddenly the "Here's a Question" project was born!

The purpose of this book is to unlock the dialogue many families struggle to engage in. We live in a culture that moves us toward isolation and concealment. Our goal is to see families break the trend and grow closer through great conversations. Children express themselves in many ways, they are all different. But unlocking a great conversation can sometimes be challenging.

These questions are designed to make your family laugh and enjoy quality time around the dinner table, riding in the car or anywhere you spend time together. Each question is accompanied by a cartoon adding humor and context to the questions. The questions are simple but can unlock deeper conversations with follow-up questions like, "Why do you think that?" "But what about this?" and so on.

Our hope is that your quality time will be enhanced and that your family will enjoy sharing, laughing, and learning about each other. Once asking questions becomes a routine, those hard questions parents need to ask will become a lot easier. We hope this book brings many enjoyable moments and brings you closer together.

Scott Bowen
Founder, Here's a Question

WHAT WOULD YOU BUY IF MONEY REALLY DID GROW ON TREES?

001

WHY IS YOUR HEART SAD WHEN FRIENDS ARE MEAN?

WHAT DO YOU THINK YOU WILL LOOK LIKE IN 20 YEARS?

WHO WILL BE THE HERO OF YOUR LIFE?

DO YOU THINK YOU WILL EVER HAVE A FRIEND ON ANOTHER CONTINENT?

THIRTY YEARS FROM NOW, WHAT CITY WILL YOU LIVE IN?

IS HEAVEN A REAL PLACE?

WHAT IS ONE THING YOU WOULD CHANGE IF YOU WERE PRESIDENT?

HOW WOULD YOUR LIFE CHANGE IF YOU NEVER MADE A BAD CHOICE?

WHAT WOULD LIFE BE LIKE IF YOU WERE FAMOUS?

WHAT WOULD HAPPEN IF YOUR GREATEST FEAR CAME TRUE?

011

WHAT WOULD HAPPEN IF YOUR GREATEST DREAM CAME TRUE?

WHAT THINGS WOULD YOU DO IF YOU WERE NEVER EMBARRASSED?

WHAT IS THE FIRST THING YOU WOULD DO IF YOU WERE THE ONE TO DISCOVER THE NEW WORLD?

WHAT WOULD YOU DO IF YOU WERE NEVER AFRAID?

015

HOW WOULD YOU FEEL IF YOU WERE UNSURE THAT YOU WOULD EAT TODAY?

WHY DO YOU THINK PEOPLE ARE DIFFERENT COLORS?

WHY DO YOU THINK PEOPLE DON'T ALWAYS AGREE WITH YOU?

WHY DO BAD CHOICES SOMETIMES SEEM BETTER THAN GOOD CHOICES?

IS THE EARTH THE ONLY PLANET WITH LIFE?

WHY ARE PEOPLE WILLING TO DIE FOR WHAT THEY BELIEVE?

021

WHAT WOULD MOTIVATE YOU TO CHEAT ON A TEST?

WHAT IS YOUR FAVORITE CHILDHOOD MEMORY?

WHAT WOULD IT BE LIKE IF YOU DIDN'T HAVE A HOME TO COME TO?

AFTER YOU DIE, HOW WILL PEOPLE SAY YOUR LIFE INFLUENCED THEM?

WHAT KIND OF PERSON DO YOU THINK YOU WILL MARRY?

WHAT WOULD YOUR LIFE BE LIKE WITHOUT SOCIAL MEDIA?

WHY DOES IT FEEL GOOD TO GIVE TO OTHERS IN NEED?

WHY DO YOU THINK WE OFTEN HURT THE PEOPLE WHO ARE CLOSEST TO US?

029

WHY DO YOU THINK WE ARE SOMETIMES UNHAPPY WITH THE WAY WE WERE MADE?

WHAT SUPERHERO WOULD YOU LIKE TO BE?

WHAT IS THE BEST THING ABOUT YOU?

WHAT QUALITIES DO YOU REALLY ADMIRE IN YOUR BEST FRIEND?

IF YOU WERE GIVEN THREE WISHES, WHAT WOULD THEY BE?

WHAT CHEERS YOU UP WHEN YOU ARE SAD?

WHAT IS ONE THING YOU WOULD CHANGE ABOUT YOURSELF?

IF YOU COULD DESIGN YOUR OWN HOUSE, WHAT WOULD IT LOOK LIKE?

WHAT IS ONE THING YOU WILL NEVER DO WHEN DISCIPLINING YOUR KIDS?

WHAT IS ONE THING YOU WILL ALWAYS DO WHEN DISCIPLINING YOUR KIDS?

039

WHAT IS YOUR FAVORITE FAMILY MEMORY FROM THE LAST MONTH?

WHAT CAR WOULD YOU LIKE TO DRIVE FOR ONE DAY?

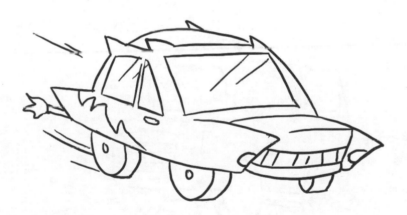

WHAT CAR WOULD YOU LIKE TO DRIVE EVERY DAY FOR 10 YEARS?

WHAT WOULD IT FEEL LIKE TO BE A LOST DOG?

AT WHAT AGE DO YOU THINK YOU WILL FALL IN LOVE?

WHAT IS THE NICEST THING YOU CAN DO FOR SOMEONE ELSE?

WHAT WOULD YOUR LIFE BE LIKE WITHOUT A CELL PHONE?

WHICH OF YOUR DREAMS WILL COME TRUE?

WHY DOES DIVORCE STINK?

WHAT MAKES KIDS SO MEAN?

HOW WOULD YOU DESCRIBE YOURSELF TO A STRANGER?

WHY ARE THERE SO MANY BAD STORIES ON THE NIGHTLY NEWS?

WHAT PROFESSIONAL SPORT WOULD YOU LIKE TO PLAY?

WHAT CAREER WILL GIVE YOU THE MOST TIME TO BE WITH YOUR FAMILY?

053

WHY ARE SOME KIDS POPULAR IN SCHOOL AND OTHERS ARE NOT?

AT WHAT AGE WILL YOU GET MARRIED?

WHAT WOULD IT BE LIKE IF YOU COULD FLY?

WHAT MAKES YOU LAUGH THE MOST?

IF IT WERE FREAKY FRIDAY, WHO WOULD YOU WANT TO SWAP PLACES WITH?

WOULD YOU TELL ON A FRIEND IF HE OR SHE STOLE SOMETHING?

059

WHAT IS YOUR PURPOSE ON THIS EARTH?

WHAT TIME PERIOD IN THE FUTURE WOULD YOU GO TO IF YOU COULD ACCESS TIME TRAVEL?

WHERE WILL YOU GO TO COLLEGE?

WHAT IS THE BEST WAY TO BE FRIENDS WITH PEOPLE WHO HAVE DIFFERENT OPINIONS?

WHY IS IT HARD TO ADMIT WHEN YOU ARE WRONG?

WHAT ARE YOU REALLY GOOD AT?

WHY IS IT HARD TO APOLOGIZE?

WHAT MAKES YOUR PARENTS PROUD OF YOU?

WHICH CELEBRITY WOULD YOU LOVE TO MEET?

WHICH BAD HABIT WILL YOU LEARN FROM YOUR MOM?

WHICH BAD HABIT WILL YOU LEARN FROM YOUR DAD?

HOW WOULD YOU ACT IF YOU WERE ABLE TO MEET YOUR SPORTS HERO?

IN WHAT WAYS ARE YOU SUPER SMART?

WHY DOES YOUR BODY NEED FOOD AND WATER?

073

WHAT CHANGES WOULD YOU MAKE IN YOUR LIFE IF YOU KNEW YOU HAD 24 HOURS TO LIVE?

WHAT WOULD IT BE LIKE TO LOSE YOUR VISION?

WHAT IS THE TOTAL NUMBER OF FRIENDS YOU WILL HAVE IN YOUR LIFE?

HOW WILL YOU INFLUENCE HISTORY?

HOW MUCH MONEY DO YOU NEED IN LIFE?

WHAT WOULD IT BE LIKE TO HAVE A FOSTER CHILD STAYING IN YOUR HOME?

WHAT MAKES YOU CRY THE MOST?

WOULD YOU STEAL SOMETHING IF NO ONE WOULD EVER KNOW?

WOULD YOU RATHER SIT ON THE FRONT ROW OR THE BACK ROW OF THE CLASSROOM?

WHAT WILL BE WRITTEN ON YOUR TOMBSTONE?

HOW WOULD YOU REACT IF YOUR BEST FRIEND OFFERED YOU ALCOHOL?

WOULD YOU EVER WANT TO LIVE IN A DIFFERENT COUNTRY?

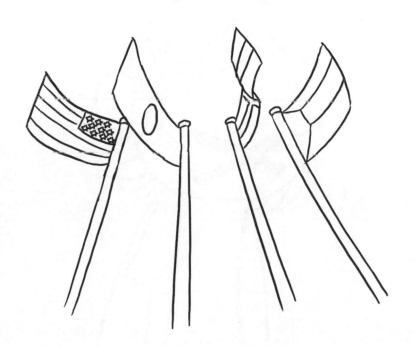

WHAT WOULD IT BE LIKE TO BE SILENT FOR AN ENTIRE DAY?

WHAT MAKES YOU REALLY ANGRY?

087

WHAT BREAKS YOUR HEART?

WILL YOU LIVE WITH YOUR PARENTS AFTER COLLEGE?

WHAT WOULD IT BE LIKE IF YOUR BROTHER OR SISTER WERE FAMOUS?

WHAT IS ONE THING YOU WOULD REMOVE FROM THE SHELVES IN THE SUPERMARKET?

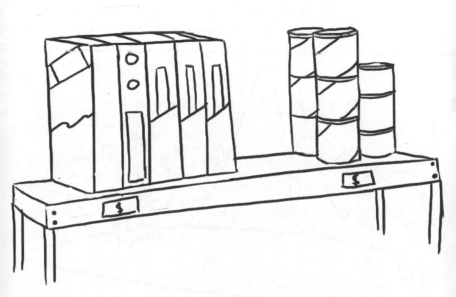

091

WHAT TIME PERIOD IN THE PAST WOULD YOU GO TO IF YOU COULD ACCESS TIME TRAVEL?

HOW OLD WILL YOU BE WHEN YOU DIE?

HOW MANY BOOKS WILL YOU READ IN YOUR LIFETIME?

WHICH DO YOU PREFER...1,000 SOCIAL MEDIA FRIENDS OR ONE TRUE FRIEND?

HOW MANY HOURS OF TV WILL YOU WATCH IN YOUR LIFETIME?

HOW TALL WILL YOU BE?

DO YOU LIKE TO MAKE QUICK DECISIONS, OR DO YOU LIKE TO TAKE YOUR TIME?

TAKE 1

HOW MANY KIDS WILL YOU HAVE?

WHY, AT A CERTAIN AGE, ARE YOU EMBARRASSED TO BE NAKED?

DESCRIBE THE DAY WHEN WE HAVE FLYING CARS?

WHY DOES IT FEEL GOOD TO HIT YOUR BROTHER OR SISTER?

WHY DO HUGS FEEL SO GOOD?

WHAT WILL YOUR LIFE BE LIKE IF YOU DON'T GET AN EDUCATION?

DO YOUR ACTIONS MAKE A DIFFERENCE AS TO WHERE YOU WILL BE AFTER YOU DIE?

WHY DOES IT FEEL SO GOOD TO WIN THE BIG GAME?

WHEN HAVE YOU BEEN THE MOST SURPRISED?

DOES IT MATTER IF WE WASTE THINGS?

WHICH ANIMAL WOULD YOU LIKE TO BE FOR A DAY?

WHAT IS YOUR FAVORITE HOUR OF THE DAY?

WHAT WOULD BE THE TITLE OF YOUR AUTOBIOGRAPHY?

WHAT IS THE WEIRDEST THING ABOUT YOU?

WHAT WOULD OTHER PEOPLE SAY IS THE WEIRDEST THING ABOUT YOU?

WOULD YOU RATHER TAKE A MATH TEST OR WRITE A PAPER?

WHAT WOULD IT BE LIKE TO TELL YOUR SISTER OR BROTHER WHY HE OR SHE IS GREAT?

WHAT SOUNDS DO YOU HEAR WHILE SLEEPING IN A TENT?

WHEN AND WHERE DO YOU FEEL MOST COMFORTABLE TALKING TO YOUR PARENTS?

WHY DO WE HIDE THE THINGS WE'VE DONE WRONG?

HOW DO YOU THINK YOU ARE GOING TO MAKE A LIVING?

WHAT MAKES YOU REALLY HAPPY?

WHY DO PEOPLE SPEAK DIFFERENT LANGUAGES?

WHAT WOULD IT BE LIKE IF YOU NEVER CLEANED YOUR ROOM?

HOW WOULD YOU REACT IF YOU HAD TO MOVE TO A DIFFERENT STATE?

WHAT WOULD IT BE LIKE IF YOU NEVER BRUSHED YOUR HAIR?

WHAT IS THE NICEST THING YOU CAN SAY TO SOMEONE?

WHAT WOULD IT BE LIKE IF YOUR PARENTS WERE MOVIE STARS?

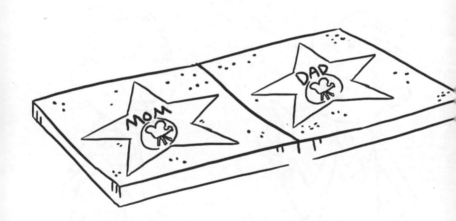

WHAT IS THE ONE THING YOU ARE MOST PROUD OF?

WHAT TWO ANIMALS WOULD YOU COMBINE TO MAKE A SUPER ANIMAL?

IF YOU COULD WRITE A SONG, WHAT WOULD THE TITLE BE?

WHAT IS THE MOST IMPORTANT RULE IN YOUR HOUSE?

WHY ARE THINGS OKAY FOR YOUR PARENTS TO SAY BUT NOT OKAY FOR YOU TO SAY?

WHY DO PEOPLE LET FAILURES IN THEIR PASTS RUIN THEIR FUTURES?

WHAT WOULD YOU SAY IF THE WHOLE WORLD HAD TO LISTEN TO YOU FOR 30 SECONDS?

WHAT WILL MAKE YOU HAPPY WHEN YOU ARE 20?

WHAT WILL MAKE YOU HAPPY WHEN YOU ARE 40?

WHAT WILL MAKE YOU HAPPY WHEN YOU ARE 60?

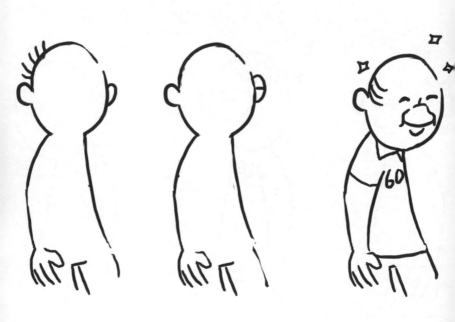

WHAT CHANGES WOULD YOU MAKE IN YOUR LIFE IF YOU KNEW YOU COULD NOT DIE?

137

WHAT TWO WORDS DESCRIBE YOU BEST?

WHAT WILL MATTER MOST TO YOU WHEN YOU ARE 90 YEARS OLD?

139

HOW WOULD YOUR MOM FEEL IF YOU GAVE HER A HUG EVERY DAY?

HOW WOULD YOUR DAD FEEL IF YOU TEXTED HIM AN "I LOVE YOU :-)" EVERY DAY?

WHAT WOULD YOU TRY IF YOU KNEW YOU WOULD NOT FAIL?

WHAT CAN YOU TEACH SOMEONE ELSE?

WHAT IS THE BEST THING YOUR MOM CAN DO FOR YOU?

WHAT IS THE BEST THING YOUR DAD CAN DO FOR YOU?

WHAT ARE YOU GOING TO BE FOR HALLOWEEN?

WHY DO WE GET ANGRY OVER THINGS THAT DON'T MATTER?

HOW FAR COULD YOU WALK?

IS IT POSSIBLE TO LEARN FROM OUR MISTAKES?

IS IT POSSIBLE TO LEARN FROM OUR SUCCESSES?

HOW MANY LANGUAGES CAN YOU LEARN?

HOW WOULD THE WORLD BE DIFFERENT IF MONEY WAS NEVER INVENTED?

WHAT WOULD YOU LEARN IF YOU MOVED TO A NEIGHBORHOOD COMPRISED OF PEOPLE FROM A DIFFERENT CULTURE?

WHAT WILL COMPUTERS BE ABLE TO DO IN 50 YEARS?

154

WHAT MAKES YOU SCARED?

WHAT WILL YOU NAME YOUR NEXT PET?

WHY DON'T PEOPLE EAT WHAT IS BEST FOR THEM?

WHY DON'T PEOPLE EXERCISE?

WHY WOULD PEOPLE RATHER SEND A MESSAGE THAN HAVE A CONVERSATION?

159

WHAT WOULD IT BE LIKE TO LOSE YOUR HEARING?

WHY ARE GIRLS GROSS AT 7 AND AMAZING AT 17?

WHY ARE BOYS GROSS AT 7 AND AMAZING AT 17?

DO WORDS HURT MORE THAN STICKS AND STONES?

WHY IS IT EASIER TO BE SELFISH THAN GENEROUS?

IF YOU WERE TO JUMP FROM A HIGH DIVE, WOULD YOU RATHER BE THE FIRST TO TRY IT OR WOULD YOU WAIT FOR OTHERS TO GO?

165

WHY IS THINKING THE BEST ABOUT A PERSON NOT ALWAYS OUR FIRST THOUGHT?

WHAT WOULD THE WORLD LOOK LIKE IF, FOR ONE DAY, EVERYONE PUT SOMEONE ELSE'S NEEDS FIRST?

WHAT PUTS YOU IN A BAD MOOD?

WHAT PUTS YOU IN A GOOD MOOD?

SHOULD YOUR PARENTS ADOPT A CHILD?

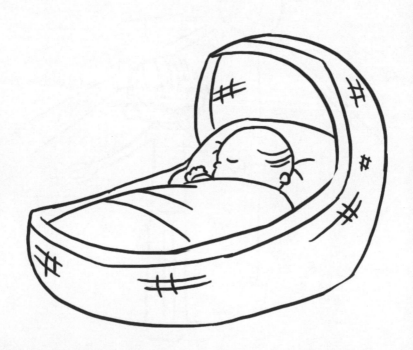

HOW DO YOU FEEL WHEN YOU SEE SOMEONE YOU LOVE SICK?

WHY DO SOME PEOPLE HAVE FAR MORE THAN THEY NEED AND OTHERS HAVE NOTHING?

WHY DO FLOWERS MAKE YOU FEEL GOOD?

WHAT WOULD IT BE LIKE TO BE IN THE ROYAL FAMILY?

WHY CAN BOYS HAVE HAIR ON THEIR LEGS AND GIRLS HAVE TO SHAVE?

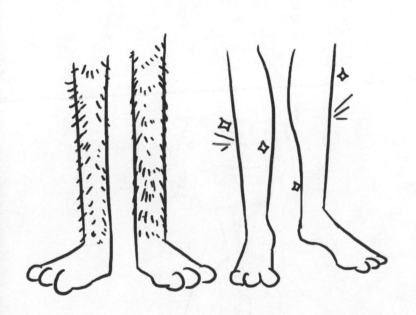

WHAT WILL OUR CLOTHES LOOK LIKE IN 25 YEARS?

WILL THERE EVER BE WORLD PEACE?

WHAT WOULD IT BE LIKE TO BE ANOTHER ETHNICITY?

WHAT IS THE DIFFERENCE BETWEEN A MISTAKE AND A BAD CHOICE?

WHAT WOULD IT BE LIKE IF ALL YOUR SIBLINGS SPOKE DIFFERENT LANGUAGES?

WHAT IS THE BEST THING YOU CAN PUT IN YOUR BODY?

WHAT WOULD YOU DO IF GRAVITY STOPPED WORKING?

WHAT WOULD LIFE BE LIKE IF PEOPLE DIDN'T HAVE CONSEQUENCES TO THEIR ACTIONS?

IF YOU COULD PUT UP A BILLBOARD, WHAT WOULD IT SAY AND WHERE WOULD IT BE?

IF YOU COULD GO BACK IN TIME 10 YEARS, WHAT ADVICE WOULD YOU GIVE YOURSELF?

WHO IS THE MOST SUCCESSFUL PERSON YOU KNOW AND WHY?

WHAT IS A BAD HABIT YOU WOULD LIKE TO OVERCOME?

WHAT ARE TWO THINGS THAT INFLUENCE YOUR LIFE THE MOST?

WHAT IS THE ONE THING THAT INFLUENCES YOUR LIFE, BUT YOU WISH IT DIDN'T?

HOW WOULD YOU DESCRIBE THE PERFECT MORNING ROUTINE?

WHAT IS ONE THING YOU WISH YOU HAD PURSUED BUT DIDN'T?

WHAT ARE TWO WAYS YOU CAN BE MORE CREATIVE?

IF YOU COULD GIVE $100 TO ANYONE OR ANY ORGANIZATION, WHO WOULD IT BE?

WHAT IS THE EARLIEST MEMORY YOU HAVE?

WHAT IS YOUR FAVORITE GAME TO PLAY?

WHAT IS YOUR FAVORITE CHRISTMAS MOVIE?

IF YOU COULD TRANSPORT YOURSELF ANYWHERE IN THE WORLD FOR ONE HOUR, WHERE WOULD IT BE?

WHAT IS THE BEST DREAM YOU'VE EVER HAD?

WHAT SONG DO YOU SECRETLY LOVE?

WHAT ANIMAL MAKES THE COOLEST NOISE?

WHEN YOU MEET SOMEONE NEW, DO YOU ASSUME THE BEST OR THE WORST ABOUT THAT PERSON?

WHAT IS THE WORST SMELL IN THE WORLD?

WHAT IS THE BEST SMELL IN THE WORLD?

IF YOU COULD ONLY KEEP ONE ITEM FROM YOUR ROOM, WHAT WOULD IT BE?

WHAT IS THE LONGEST WALK YOU HAVE EVER TAKEN?

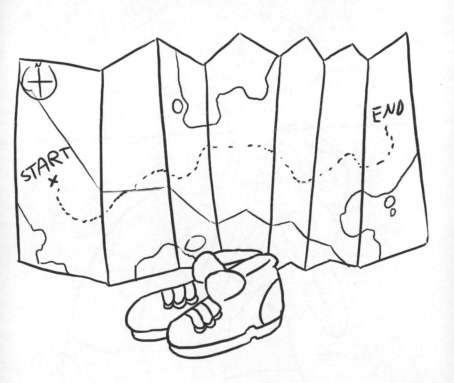

WHO WOULD YOU TRUST WITH YOUR DEEPEST SECRET?

HOW MUCH WOULD YOU PAY FOR WATER IF YOU WERE STRANDED IN THE DESERT?

207

HOW MANY IS TOO MANY FRIENDS?

WHY DOES IT HURT PEOPLE WHEN WE ARE SELFISH?

WHAT SHOULD THE SPEED LIMIT BE ON THE HIGHWAY?

HOW WOULD YOU FEEL IF YOU ENCOURAGED EVERY PERSON YOU ENCOUNTERED TODAY?

HOW WOULD YOU FEEL IF EVERYONE YOU ENCOUNTERED TODAY ENCOURAGED YOU?

WHAT IS ONE WORD OR PHRASE THAT YOU USE TOO OFTEN?

WHAT IS LOVE?

WHY DO YOU LIKE RECEIVING GIFTS?

IS UNDERWEAR REALLY NECESSARY?

WHAT IS PREVENTING YOU FROM INVENTING SOMETHING?

HOW DO YOU MAKE PEOPLE FEEL SPECIAL?

HOW MANY PAIRS OF SHOES WILL YOU BUY IN YOUR LIFETIME?

HOW MANY CANDY BARS WILL YOU EAT IN YOUR LIFETIME?

WHEN ARE YOU MOST DISGUSTED?

PLOP!

WOULD YOU EVER JUMP OUT OF AN AIRPLANE?

HOW WOULD YOUR LIFE BE DIFFERENT IF YOU HAD TO WALK A MILE TO FETCH WATER?

223

HOW MANY IDEAS CAN YOUR BRAIN HOLD?

HAVE YOU EVER FELT LIKE YOU WERE INVISIBLE? IF SO, WHEN?

WHAT IS THE MOST DISAPPOINTED YOU HAVE EVER BEEN?

IF YOU COULD CHANGE YOUR GIVEN NAME, WHAT WOULD YOU CHANGE IT TO?

HELLO, MY NAME IS:

Lord Tigerzilla the III

WHAT IS ONE WAY PEOPLE KNOW YOU ARE HAPPY?

WHAT IS ONE WAY PEOPLE KNOW YOU ARE SAD?

WHAT IS ONE THING YOU WOULD NEVER SELL, NO MATTER THE PRICE?

WHICH WOULD YOU RATHER BE...A SCIENTIST OR AN ARTIST? WHY?

HOW MANY TVS WOULD YOU LIKE TO HAVE IN YOUR HOUSE?

232

WHAT IS ONE MOVIE YOU ARE SCARED TO WATCH?

CHINCHILAZILLA!!

TELL ABOUT A TIME WHEN SOMEONE MADE FUN OF YOU.

WHAT COULD BRING YOU TO HIT A TOTAL STRANGER?

235

WHAT COULD BRING YOU TO HIT YOUR SIBLING?

WHO MAKES YOU LAUGH WHEN YOU SEE HIS OR HER FACE?

237

WHAT WOULD IT BE LIKE IF YOU NEVER BRUSHED YOUR TEETH?

HOW DO OTHER PEOPLE DESCRIBE YOU TO THEIR FRIENDS?

WOULD YOU RATHER HAVE ONE LOVING FRIEND FOREVER OR $5,000,000?

WOULD YOU RATHER GO FOR A BIKE RIDE OR PLAY A VIDEO GAME?

WOULD YOU RATHER GO TO A PARTY OR HAVE ONE FRIEND OVER?

WOULD YOU KEEP A FRIEND'S SECRET IF YOU KNEW HE OR SHE NEEDED HELP?

243

WHAT UNIQUE GIFT DO YOU POSSESS?

IF YOU COULD START A NEW FAMILY TRADITION, WHAT WOULD IT BE?

WHAT CHARACTER IN A BOOK OR MOVIE WOULD YOU LIKE TO HAVE AS YOUR BEST FRIEND?

WHAT THREE WORDS WOULD YOU USE TO DESCRIBE YOUR MOTHER?

ACROSS:
1. Mom is ____
3. Mom is ____

DOWN:
2. Mom is ____

WHAT THREE WORDS WOULD YOU USE TO DESCRIBE YOUR FATHER?

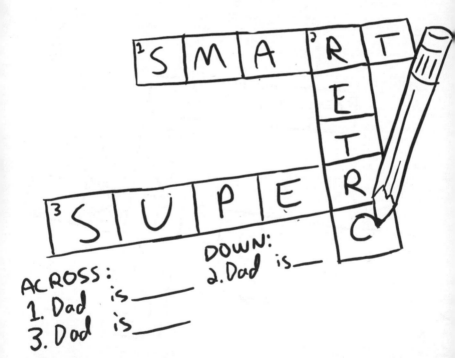

ACROSS:
1. Dad is ____
3. Dad is ____

DOWN:
2. Dad is ____

HOW WOULD YOU DESCRIBE THE PERFECT SCHOOL?

HOW WOULD YOU DESCRIBE THE PERFECT TEACHER?

IF YOU HAD ALL THE TIME IN THE WORLD, WHAT WOULD YOU DO?

HOW MUCH MONEY DO YOU WANT TO HAVE BEFORE YOU RETIRE?

WHAT IS YOUR PROUDEST MOMENT?

HOW DO YOU KNOW WHAT IS RIGHT OR WRONG?

WHAT IS ONE CHALLENGE YOUR GRANDCHILDREN WILL FACE?

IF YOU COULD SMELL ONE THING FIRST THING IN THE MORNING, WHAT WOULD IT BE?

HAVE YOU EVER LIED TO A FRIEND?

257

WHAT WOULD YOU DO IF YOU SAW A MAN TAKE A WOMAN'S PURSE?

WHEN YOU MEET A NEW PERSON, ARE YOU MORE LIKELY TO ASK A QUESTION OR ANSWER A QUESTION?

WHAT ARE TWO ADJECTIVES YOU'D LIKE PEOPLE TO USE WHEN DESCRIBING YOU?

WHERE WILL YOU CELEBRATE YOUR BIRTHDAY IN FIVE YEARS?

WHAT WOULD IT BE LIKE IF YOU DIDN'T HAVE A FAMILY TO COME HOME TO?

HOW MANY OTHER GALAXIES ARE THERE IN THE UNIVERSE?

WHO DO YOU KNOW THAT IS TERRIBLE AT KEEPING SECRETS?

WHAT QUALITIES ARE IN A TRUE FRIEND?

WHO WILL BE A PART OF YOUR MOST FAVORITE MEMORY?

WHAT HAPPENS IF YOU BREAK A RULE AT HOME?

WHY DO WE OFTEN TREAT PEOPLE WHO ARE DIFFERENT FROM US DIFFERENTLY?

WHAT WILL YOUR FACE LOOK LIKE WHEN YOU ARE 80?

WHO DO YOU THINK YOU WILL LOVE THE MOST IN YOUR LIFE?

WHAT CAN YOU DO ABOUT PEOPLE IN YOUR COMMUNITY WHO MAY NOT EAT A MEAL TODAY?

IF YOU WERE WITHOUT ELECTRICITY, WHAT ARE THE STEPS YOU WOULD TAKE TO PREPARE A MEAL?

272

WHAT IS THE FIRST THING YOU WOULD DO IF YOU WON THE LOTTERY?

HOW BIG WILL YOUR EARS WILL BE WHEN YOU ARE 80? WHAT ABOUT YOUR NOSE?

HOW MANY MILES DO YOU THINK YOU CAN RUN?

0.1 MILE

DO YOU PREFER TEAM SPORTS OR INDIVIDUAL SPORTS?

WHAT ARE TWO THINGS YOU THINK YOUR PARENTS ARE THANKFUL FOR?

WHAT ARE TWO THINGS YOU LOVE ABOUT THE PERSON TO YOUR RIGHT?

IS THE BIBLE TRUE? HOW DO YOU KNOW?

WHAT'S THE BEST GIFT YOU COULD GET FOR CHRISTMAS?

WHAT'S THE BEST GIFT YOU COULD GIVE FOR CHRISTMAS?

281

WOULD YOU RATHER SPEND A WEEK IN THE MOUNTAINS OR AT THE BEACH?

HOW WOULD YOUR LIFE CHANGE IF YOU WOULD NEVER TELL A LIE?

283

WHAT IS THE BEST MEAL YOUR MOM MAKES?

WHAT IS THE BEST MEAL YOUR DAD MAKES?

WHAT IS MORE IMPORTANT TO YOU...WINNING A GAME OR MAKING FRIENDS?

WHAT IS YOUR FAVORITE CHRISTMAS TRADITION?

WHAT CAN YOU LEARN FROM THE ELDERLY?

WHAT ARE SOME WAYS TO THANK A SERVICE MEMBER?

WOULD YOU RATHER BE ONSTAGE OR BACKSTAGE?

HOW WOULD YOU COMPLETE THIS STATEMENT? I FEEL SPECIAL WHEN PEOPLE...

291

WHAT IS THE WORST THING YOU CAN PUT IN YOUR BODY?

HOW DO YOU REACT WHEN YOU ACCOMPLISH A GOAL?

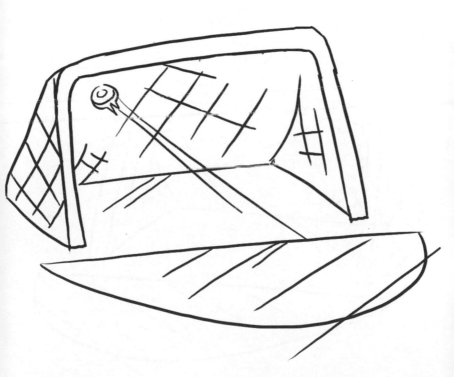

HOW DO YOU REACT WHEN YOU FAIL TO REACH A GOAL?

PLINK

DO YOU LIKE A ROUTINE SCHEDULE OR DO YOU PREFER TO GO WITH THE FLOW?

HOW MANY TOYS ARE CURRENTLY UNDER YOUR BED?

KEEP OUT!
SECRET FORT

IF YOU HAD $100, HOW MANY DOLLARS WOULD YOU GIVE AWAY?

WHAT ACTIVITY TAKES THE MOST COURAGE?

DO MOST OF YOUR FRIENDS DO THE RIGHT THINGS OR THE WRONG THINGS?

WHAT IS YOUR FAVORITE CARTOON?

HOW IMPORTANT IS HAVING A CLEAN APPEARANCE? WHY?

IF YOU FOUNDED A NEW COUNTRY, WHAT WOULD YOU NAME IT? WHAT WOULD THE FLAG LOOK LIKE?

HOW MANY SODAS WILL YOU DRINK IN YOUR LIFETIME?

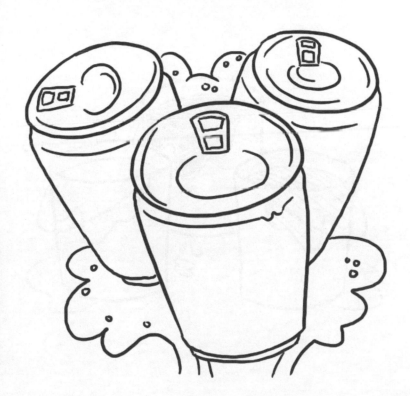

WHAT COLOR WOULD YOU PAINT YOUR ROOM IF YOU WERE ALLOWED?

IF YOU COULD GIVE EVERYONE ON THE PLANET ONE THING, WHAT WOULD IT BE?

305

WHY DOES THE TRUTH HURT SOMETIMES?

AT WHAT HAVE YOU WORKED HARD AND ACCOMPLISHED?

WHEN ARE YOU MOST NERVOUS?

WHEN DO YOU HAVE THE HIGHEST LEVEL OF ANTICIPATION?

WHERE IS ONE PLACE YOU WOULD LIKE TO TRAVEL THIS YEAR?

WHAT PEOPLE GROUP DO YOU FIND THE MOST INTRIGUING?

SHOULD EVERYTHING IN LIFE BE FAIR? WHY?

WHY DO WE COLLECT THINGS THAT WILL EVENTUALLY END UP IN THE TRASH?

WHAT IS YOUR FUNNIEST JOKE?

IF YOU HAD TO EAT THE SAME LUN(H EVERY DAY, WHAT WOULD IT BE?

WHAT IS THE MOST DIFFICULT THING ABOUT BEING YOUR AGE?

WHAT WOULD YOU DO IF YOU COULD CONTROL TIME?

WOULD YOU RATHER HAVE A SURPRISE PARTY OR A PLANNED PARTY?

WOULD YOU RATHER SCARE SOMEONE OR BE SCARED?

WHAT EMOTIONS DO YOU FEEL WHEN YOU SEE SOMEONE BEING CRUEL TO ANOTHER PERSON OR ANIMAL?

320

WHAT IS ONE THING YOU ARE ENVIOUS OF?

WHAT IS ONE THING YOU THINK PEOPLE ENVY ABOUT YOU?

WHY DO YOU THINK IT FEELS WEIRD TO HAVE NO CLOTHES ON IN PUBLIC?

WHAT IS ONE PIECE OF TECHNOLOGY YOU THINK SHOULD BE INVENTED?

WHAT WOULD IT BE LIKE IF YOU SLEPT WITH YOUR FAMILY ON A DIRT FLOOR?

WHO MAKES YOU FEEL THE MOST SPECIAL?

WILL YOU EVER HAVE A MENTOR?

327

WILL YOU EVER MENTOR ANYONE?
IF SO, WHO?

IS THERE SOMEONE YOU FEEL LIKE SENDING A NOTE TO? DO IT!

IF YOU COULD SEND YOURSELF A LETTER THAT YOU WOULD RECEIVE IN 10 YEARS, WHAT WOULD IT SAY?

TELL YOUR LIFE STORY IN SEVEN WORDS OR LESS.

WHAT IS THE GREATEST ADVENTURE YOU HAVE EVER HAD?

WHAT IS YOUR FAVORITE WAY TO CELEBRATE?

WHAT WOULD YOU DO IF YOU WERE INVISIBLE FOR A DAY?

DO YOU EVER FEEL LONELY? IF SO, WHEN?

WHAT ARE TWO WAYS YOU MIGHT DISAPPOINT YOUR PARENTS?

HAVE YOU EVER LOST SOMEONE YOU LOVED?

337

DO YOU EVER HAVE FOMO (FEAR OF MISSING OUT)?

HOW DO YOU FEEL WHEN SOMEONE IS UPSET WITH YOU?

WOULD YOU RATHER CREATE AN IDEA OR SOLVE A PROBLEM?

WHAT'S THE BEST WAY TO PASS THE TIME ON A LONG ROAD TRIP?

DO OUTWARD LOOKS MATTER?

WHAT WOULD YOU DO IF YOU GOT LOST FROM YOUR FAMILY?

IF YOU COULD START YOUR OWN NATIONAL HOLIDAY, WHAT WOULD IT BE IN CELEBRATION OF?

HAPPY FREE KITTENS DAY!

WHAT IS SOMETHING YOU'VE SAID THAT YOU WISH YOU COULD UNSAY?

WHAT IS SOMETHING YOU'VE SEEN THAT YOU WISH YOU COULD UNSEE?

WHAT OLYMPIC EVENT WOULD YOU LIKE TO COMPETE IN?

WHAT IS YOUR FAVORITE THING TO DO IN THE SUMMER?

WHAT IS YOUR FAVORITE THING TO DO IN THE WINTER?

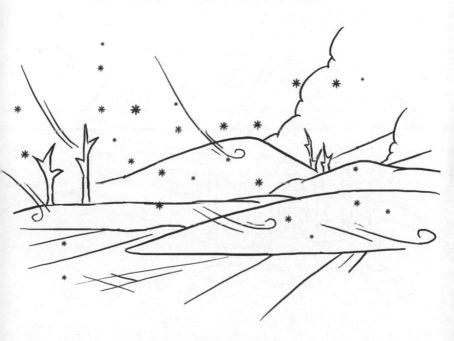

WHAT IS THE BEST THING YOU HAVE EVER CONSTRUCTED?

WHY IS IT BAD FOR YOUR BRAIN TO WATCH TOO MUCH TV?

351

HOW WOULD YOUR ACTIONS AND WORDS CHANGE IF YOU WERE FOLLOWED AROUND 24/7 BY A TV CREW?

WHAT ARE TWO WAYS YOU COULD LOSE A FRIEND?

WHAT ARE TWO WAYS YOU COULD GAIN A FRIEND?

WHAT EMOTIONS DO YOU FEEL WHEN YOUR PARENTS DISCIPLINE YOU?

355

WHAT IS UNCONDITIONAL LOVE?

WHICH IS MORE IMPORTANT TO YOU, HAVING A BIG HOUSE OR A BIG YARD?